BUILD YOUR OWN BACKYARD

BIRDHOUSES

and FEEDERS

First published in 2011 by Cool Springs Press, an imprint of the Quayside
Publishing Group, P.O. Box 2828, Brentwood, TN 37024 USA.

The information in this book is true and complete to the best of our knowledge. All
recommendations are made without any guarantee on the part of the author or Publisher, who
also disclaims any liability incurred in connection with the use of this data or specific details.

We recognize, further, that some words, model names, and designations mentioned herein are
the property of the trademark holder. We use them for identification purposes only. This is not
an official publication.

Cool Springs Press titles are also available at discounts in bulk quantity for industrial or
sales-promotional use. For details write to Special Sales Manager at Cool Springs Press, P.O.
Box 2828, Brentwood, TN 37024 USA.

EAN: 978-159186-011-2

First Printing 2011
1 2 3 4 5

Library of Congress Cataloging-in-Publication Data

Build your own backyard birdhouses and feeders / edited by Ken Beck.
    p. cm.
 ISBN 978-1-59186-011-2 (alk. paper)
 1. Birdhouses--Design and construction. 2. Bird feeders--Design and
construction. I. Beck, Ken, 1951-QL676.5.B848 2011
690'.8927--dc23
                                                2011016803

Managing Editor: Billie Brownell
Art Director: Bill Kersey, KerseyGraphics

Visit the Cool Springs Press website at www.coolspringspress.com

Photography and Illustration Credits
All illustrations are by Bill Kersey, KerseyGraphics

All photographs provided by Brian Small with the exceptions of the Tree Swallow
(page 43, iStock) and pages 7, 8, 9 (Thinkstock).

Printed in China

BUILD YOUR OWN BACKYARD
BIRDHOUSES
and FEEDERS

Edited by Ken Beck

COOL SPRINGS PRESS

Growing Successful Gardeners™

www.coolspringspress.com

BRENTWOOD, TENNESSEE

Contents

Feeders

Introduction

You can always buy a birdhouse or a feeder, but making one with your own hands is sure to increase the joys of creating a nurturing environment for the birds that you love. Plus, well-built and well-placed birdhouses and bird feeders can bring homeowners hours of pleasure for many years.

There are dozens, perhaps even *hundreds*, of different birdhouse and feeder designs and many look quite spectacular. But the truth is that birds don't look for something decorative—they just look for simple structures that work. Never let your decorative touches get in the way of good, sound design.

Good birdhouse and feeder designs must consider the bird first. If you want to attract a specific species to your backyard lawn or garden, your first step is to study and learn the needs of that particular species.

You need to find out when they arrive in the spring, the specific type of habitat they prefer, and what their feeding habits are. Most

important, you want to learn all you can about their nesting preferences. This knowledge will aid you in deciding the type of birdhouse or feeder that will work best for your chosen feathered friend.

Armed with this information, you can then decide the type of structures to construct, where to locate them, how high off the ground to mount them, the appropriate size for the entrance hole, and, if you make more than one house, how far apart you should set them.

For example, bluebird houses need a 1½-inch-diameter entrance hole, are best located in or near clearings, and should be spaced about 100 yards apart.

You also need to consider how you will place your birdhouses or feeders so that they will be secure and not succumb to the forces of nature, such as heavy rains and strong winds. Always place the entrance to your birdhouses so that they face away from the prevailing weather (wind, rain, and so forth) in your area. If most of your weather comes from the south and the west, for instance, entrances should be mounted toward the north and the east.

While fence posts may be convenient, nest boxes actually work better when they're mounted on PVC pipes or freestanding metal poles. This allows you to better adjust the height and discourage a host of predators.

Bird species that elect to live in birdhouses are basically searching for a cavity where they can nest, lay their eggs, and raise their young. They are also looking for surrounding areas that offer food, water, and other kinds of shelter.

Among the more familiar species that will nest in manmade birdhouses are bluebirds, chickadees, finches, flycatchers, hummingbirds, kestrels, nuthatches, owls, purple martins, phoebes, robins, swallows, titmice, warblers, wrens, and some species of ducks and woodpeckers.

As more wildlife habitats fall victim to progress and disappear, your birdhouse can serve an important role in conservation since it provides these birds with additional nesting options in an ever-crowded world.

Helpful Hints

1 The preferred building material for most birdhouses is redwood, western cedar, or cypress; it weathers better than pine or maple.

2 When purchasing plywood for outdoor projects, use exterior grade because it can better handle the elements. If you use untreated lumber, it will need to be painted with exterior-grade paint.

3 Hardware, such as hinges, should be brass or galvanized, and nails and screws should be rust resistant.

4 Birdhouses need ventilation and drainage holes. Feeders also need small drainage holes.

5 A table saw, hammer, screwdriver, and drill will be the most useful tools. For some projects, other tools may be needed, such as a jigsaw.

6 For drilling circular entrance holes, spade bits will do the trick. A countersink bit will allow you to insert a screw into the wood below the surface. You can fill the hole with wood filler and sand it for a smooth finish.

7 A speed square or combination square will come in handy when you're measuring angles.

8 Measure and mark all pieces for a project before you cut anything so that you use the wood efficiently.

9 Always drill a small hole, called a pilot hole, through the wood and into the second piece of wood before you screw them together. This makes it easier to insert screws and creates a tighter fit. It also helps to prevent splitting.

🔟 Lumber is sold in standard sizes that are not the same as its actual finished measurement. For example, a 1-inch × 6-inch piece is actually three-fourths inch thick × 5½ inches wide.

⑪ Never paint, stain, or treat the *inside* of birdhouses.

⑫ Think about where a birdhouse or feeder will be located in your yard before you add the base or back.

⑬ Songbirds do not need a perch on their houses; a perch will only allow predators to gain entry.

⑭ Strongly consider using a predator guard on birdhouses and feeders.

⑮ Never make birdhouses of metal; they will become much too hot in the sun.

⑯ Birdhouse walls should generally be about three-fourths inch thick.

⑰ Sloped roofs will help the water drain off more easily.

⑱ Birdhouses should be placed a minimum of four feet above the ground.

⑲ Wild birds seem to be more attracted to birdhouses painted in shades of brown, tan, or gray, which blend in with the environment.

⑳ If you paint the exterior of a birdhouse, use a water-based paint.

Wrens have a reputation of being picky builders, as they may build several nests before finishing one that they deem suitable. You'll want to set your wren house in a place that receives partial sunlight. If you can provide 3-inch-long twigs nearby, the wrens will probably use them in the construction of their nests. Mount the nest box 6 to 10 feet off the ground. Near a tree, fencerow, or shrub is best. Be sure to use some type of predator guard to keep squirrels, snakes, raccoons, and other creatures from harming the nestlings.

Materials

1" × 6" × 4' long cedar
1⅝" rust-resistant screws
Two exterior-coated nails
Two small ¹³⁄₁₆" screw eyes
3" piece of bendable wire

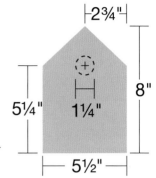

Instructions

1 Mark and cut boards to the following dimensions:
Front: 5½" × 8"
2 sides: 4" × 5¼"
Back: 5½" × 8"
Floor: 4" × 4"
Roof: 4½" × 7¾"
Roof: 5¼" × 7¾"

2 On the front piece, mark the center of the top end at 2¾". Measure and mark points 5¼" from the bottom on both edges. With a ruler, trace the line from the top center point to the side measurement on each edge. Cut on the lines to form a 45-degree angle at the peak, as shown in the diagram.

3 Repeat step 2 on the back panel.

4 On the front piece, mark a point 2½" down from the peak, centered right to left. Cut a 1¼" diameter entry hole, using the mark as the center of the circle.

5 Drill two ¼" ventilation holes 1" from the top in each side panel.

6 Position the left side against the back panel with the bottom edges flush against each other. Along the back drill pilot holes ⅜" in from the edge and insert screws to secure the side to the back.

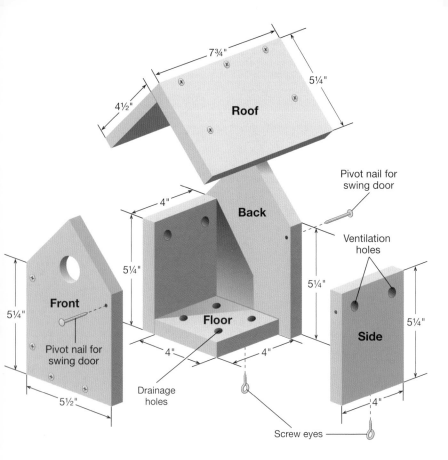

7 Drill four drainage holes through the floor. Position the floor against the back and side pieces as shown in the diagram. Drill pilot holes and secure the floor with screws.

8 Position the front panel against the floor and side, making sure the bottom edges are flush and the front and back are even. Drill pilot holes through the front panel and insert screws.

9 Pre-drill a hole and insert one screw eye in the bottom of the unattached side.

10 Position the side carefully in place and mark on the front and back panels where the pivot nails will be inserted, about 1" down from the top of the side and ⅜" in from the edge (as shown in the diagram). If using six-penny nails, drill ⅛" holes and insert the nails. You will be able to swing the door open and closed by holding onto the screw eye.

11 Mark where the second screw eye will be inserted in the floor piece as close to the side screw eye as possible. Drill a pilot hole and insert the second screw eye. Using the flexible wire, secure the two eyes together.

12 Assemble the roof as shown in the diagram, with the wider piece extending ¾" past the peak and the narrower 4½" piece at a right angle and flush against the wider one.

13 Set the roof in place with a 1¾" overhang in the front and a ½" overhang in the back. Mark where the screws will be inserted. Drill pilot holes and secure the roof with screws.

A bluebird nest box should be mounted 4 to 5 feet off the ground on a wooden post or a pole. The edge of grassy open areas such as meadows, cemeteries, golf courses, or pastures makes an ideal location. These boxes should not be posted beneath trees; however, a shrub or tree within 25 to 100 feet of the entrance makes a handy foraging perch for the adults. To protect the birds from sun and wind, place the 1½-inch entry hole facing the east or the direction opposite from which most severe weather strikes your region. Keep the box away from sites with house sparrows that may invade the house. Don't paint or stain the inside and don't put a perch on a bluebird box. Clean out the nest box after the young birds leave.

Materials

1" × 6" × 6' piece of rough-cut lumber:
    red or western cedar, poplar, pine
Exterior-coated nails
One rust-resistant screw

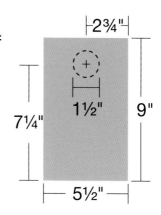

Instructions

1 Mark and cut the lumber to the
following dimensions:
Back: 5½" × 13½"
2 sides: 5½" × 9"
Front: 5½" × 9"
Roof: 5½" × 7½"
Floor: 4" × 5½"

2 Drill four ¼" drainage holes through the floor, and drill two ¼"
ventilation holes in each side piece approximately 1" from the top
edge.

3 Mark a point on the front piece 7¼" from the bottom, centered
left to right. Drill a 1½" diameter entry hole using the mark as a
centerpoint.

4 Measure and mark points 3" from the top on the front and back
sides of the back panel. Position one side panel against the back
panel with the top edge of the side on the 3" mark and the edges
flush. Nail them together using the 3" mark on the back as your
guide.

5 Position and nail the front to the side as shown in the diagram.

6 The floor piece will be recessed ½" up from the bottom edges of
the front and sides. Set the floor piece in place and nail it to the
front, side, and back panels.

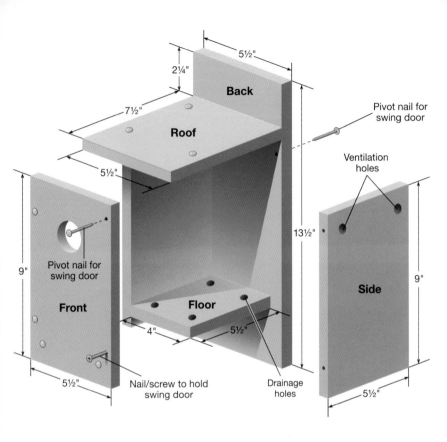

7 Set the roof in place, flush with the back panel. Nail the roof to the fixed side and front.

8 On the front panel where the side has not been attached, mark a point 1" down from the top and ⅜" in from the edge. On the back side of the back panel, mark a point 4" down from the top and ⅜" in from the edge. These are the swing door pivot points.

9 Carefully position the top of the swing door in place as shown in the diagram. Drill ⅛" holes on your marks and drive a nail into each hole. You should be able to swing the side door open and closed from the bottom.

10 With your swing door closed, drill a hole 1½" up from the bottom edge through the front panel into the side as shown in the diagram. Insert a screw to lock the door. It can be removed and the swing door opened easily for cleaning.

Migrating butterflies seek shelter during bad weather, often in the cracks of trees or building crevices. Those butterflies that hibernate over the winter months also need cover from harsh weather. A butterfly house can come to the rescue. The slits or access windows allow butterflies to come and go as they please, and they keep predators out. Decorate the butterfly house with bright colors such as red, yellow, orange, and blue. Set it on a pole two to four feet high facing south in a shady place near water and flowers.

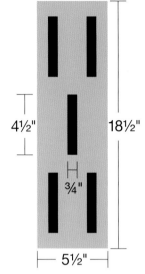
Materials

1" × 8" × 8' piece of pine lumber
Exterior-coated nails
1⅝" rust-resistant screws
Pieces of tree bark or floral moss
Exterior paint

Instructions

1 Mark and cut pine boards to the
following dimensions:
Back: 5½" × 20"
Front: 5½" × 18½"
Two sides: 6" × 20"
Floor: 7" × 6"
Roof: 7¼" × 7½"

4½"   18½"

¾"

5½"

2 On a side panel measure and mark a point 1½" from the top on
one edge. Draw a line from the opposite top corner to the mark
and cut on that line, forming a side piece 20" long on one edge
and 18½" on the other. Repeat this step with the other side panel.

3 Use one of the side pieces to mark its top angle onto the top edge
of the back panel. Bevel-cut the top edge of the back so that it
slopes forward at the same angle as the side piece.

4 Measure and mark five 4½" long by ¾" wide slits in the front
piece and stagger them, as shown in the diagram. Bore a starter
hole for the blade, and use a jigsaw to cut out the rectangles on
the lines.

5 Attach the floral moss or tree bark to the inside (the side with the
shorter beveled edge) of the back panel with nails. This will give
the butterflies something to cling to.

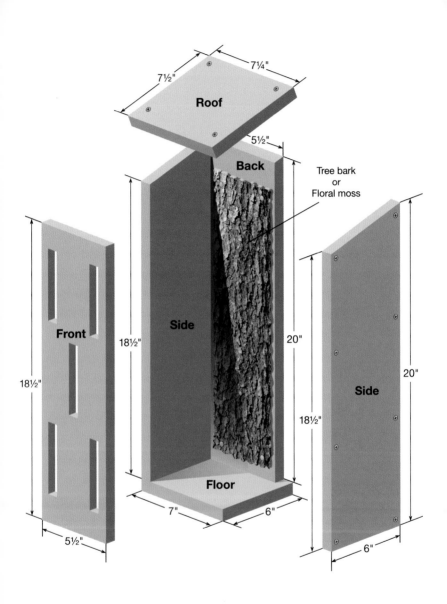

Roof

7½"

7¼"

5½"

Back

Tree bark
or
Floral moss

Front

Side

18½"

20"

18½"

5½"

Side

20"

18½"

Floor

7"

6"

6"

6 Center the back panel on top of the 7" side of the floor, ¾" in from each edge, as shown in the diagram. Drill pilot holes and secure the two pieces with screws.

7 Position one of the sides on the floor, beside the back panel, with the shorter edge in the front. Drill pilot holes and secure the side to the floor and the back panel with screws. Repeat with the other side piece.

8 Position the front panel in between the two side panels. After drilling pilot holes through the sides, secure it with screws.

9 Set the roof in place with a slight overhang in the back and front. Drill pilot holes and secure the top with screws, which will allow the top to be removed for cleaning or replacing the tree bark or moss.

10 Paint the exterior in the bright colors of your choice.

(For robins, mourning doves, phoebes, and blue jays.)

This open platform will attract a variety of birds as a nesting place when it is placed beneath shelters, eaves, or porches. The platform may be mounted 7 to 15 feet high on the side of a shed, porch, or garage that overlooks open spaces and foliage in your backyard. Choose a location that is safe from the elements, predators, and direct sunlight.

Materials

1" × 8" × 2' cedar

1⅝" rust-resistant screws

Instructions

1 From lumber cut the following pieces:

Back: 8" × 6"

2 bases: 3½" × 7"

Front mantle: 8" × 2¼"

2 At a 45-degree angle, cut the four corners off of the back to the dimensions shown. This is just a decorative touch. You don't have to be exact.

3 Mark a point 1¾" from the top of the back panel and ½" in from the left edge. Measure a 16-degree angle, as shown in the diagram, and lightly trace it on the back from the marked point to the center of the back. This is where the top edge of the left base piece will be positioned on the back.

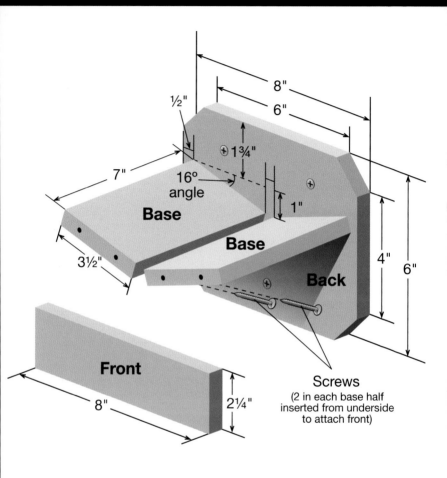

8"

6"

½"

⊕ 1¾"

7"

16°
angle

Base

Base

3½"

1"

Back

4"

6"

Front

8"

2¼"

Screws
(2 in each base half
inserted from underside
to attach front)

❹ Repeat the measurement and tracing on the right side, forming a wide-angled "V" shape.

❺ Drill two small holes ⅜" below each of the traced lines to show you where the screws will be inserted from the back.

6 Hold one base piece in place against the back panel. Drill pilot holes through those made in step 5 and into the base. Insert the screws from the back side.

7 Hold the other base piece in place. There should be a slight gap between the two. Drill pilot holes through the back and into the second base piece. Secure it to the back with screws.

8 Mount the front mantle to the angled base halves by driving screws from the underside of the bases at a steep angle.

The largest North American swallow, purple martins nest in colonies and need their birdhouses available by mid-March. The only bird species in eastern North America totally dependent on humans for nest cavities, they prefer gourd houses over any other birdhouse building material. Not only do the martins sing and fly gracefully through the air like trapeze artists, but they feast on mosquitoes, beetles, flies, wasps, flying ants, and other noxious insects. Set the mounting post about 40 to 120 feet away from your home, and take note that there should be no trees taller than the martin houses within 40 feet. Experts say the farther purple martin houses are from trees, the better.

Materials

12 dried gourds, 6" diameter minimum
1" × 2" × 24' cedar or pine for mounting
1⅝" rust-resistant screws
15' of vinyl-covered clothesline or bend-
    able wire for hanging
Fine grade sandpaper
Exterior paint and primer
18'-25' post set in an open area

Instructions

1 Measure and cut from the cedar or pine:
   Six mounting arms: 48"
   Wire: Twelve 15" lengths

2 Drill a 2" hole in the fattest part of each gourd for the entrance holes.

3 Use a stick or spoon to loosen seeds and other material in the gourd. Remove everything from inside and allow it to dry.

4 Lightly sand each gourd.

5 Brush on primer and allow it to dry before painting. Apply two coats, as this provides insulation against heat.

6 Measure and mark a centered hole 3" to 4" from each end of the 2" × 48" mounting arms. Drill ¼" holes through the marks.

7 Drill small holes on each side of the gourd's neck large enough to thread the wire through the hangers.

8 Thread one end of the wire through the holes in a gourd's neck and through the hole in the mounting arm. Twist the wire together tightly. Repeat until all 12 gourds are mounted.

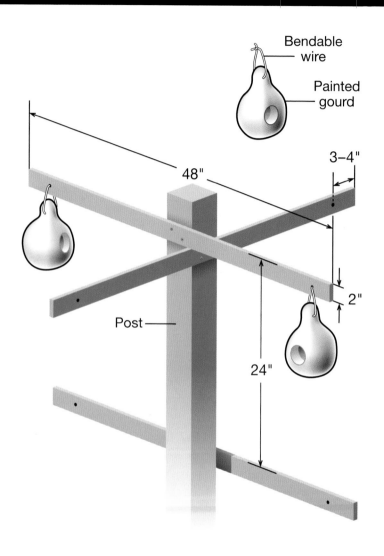

Bendable wire

Painted gourd

3–4"

48"

2"

Post

24"

9 Mount two sets of wooden arms in alternate directions, at right angles to each other, close to the top of the post.

10 Mount the second set 2' below the top set of wooden arms.

11 Mount the third set 2' below the second set of wooden arms.

12 To mount the post, dig a hole 3' to 4' deep with a post-hole digger. Erect the post, and pack gravel around it in the hole to secure it. Check the pole for plumb with a level as you backfill.

Lakes, ponds, and swamps are the natural locations for wood duck and hooded merganser nest boxes. These ducks nest from April to June. Once the young hatch from their eggs, within a day, they will use their claws to climb to the nest entrance and drop to the water or ground. If they fall to the ground, the mother will guide the ducklings to the nearest water hole. Experts recommend that these boxes be erected 6 to 8 feet over water, using wooden or steel poles with predator-proof metal cones or sleeves. You may also place boxes in a woodland habitat close to water mounted at least 20 feet high. At least three inches of mixed sawdust and wood chips should be put in the bottom of the box. The entrance hole should be facing the water. This nest box also serves the hooded merganser.

Materials

1" × 12" × 12' rough-cut cedar
4" × 16" quarter-inch galvanized hardware cloth or wire mesh
Two hinges with screws
Staples
1⅝" rust-resistant screws
Two 6" pieces of flexible wire
Four medium 1⅜" screw eyes

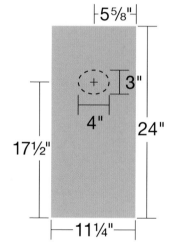

Instructions

1. Measure and cut pieces from 1" × 12" × 12' cedar as follows (all pieces are the full width of the board):
   Back: 32"
   2 sides: 24"
   Front: 24"
   Roof: 16"
   Floor: 9¾"

2. Drill four ¼" drainage holes in the floor. Drill two ¼" ventilation holes at the top of each side panel.

3. On the front panel mark a point down 6½" from the top and centered from left to right. Cut out a 3" high by 4" wide entrance hole with the marking at the center of the cut.

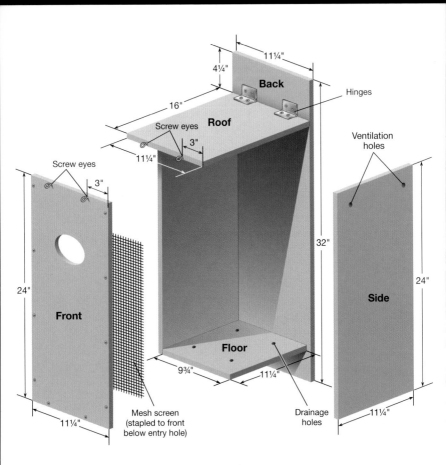

4 On the inside of the front panel, staple wire mesh starting ½"
below the entrance hole and extending down to the floor.

5 Drill evenly spaced pilot holes ⅜" from both edges of the back
panel starting 5½" from the top edge and stopping 3½" from the
bottom. Position one side panel 5" down from the top of the back
panel. Attach the side to the back using 1⅝" screws. Repeat with
the other side panel.

6 Position the floor between the two sides and flush with their bottom edges. Drill pilot holes and attach the floor to the back and sides with screws.

7 Position the front panel on top of the floor and sides with the wire mesh on the inside. Drill pilot holes and screw the front in place.

8 Set the roof in place on the box. Mark where the hinge screws pilot holes need to be drilled. Attach the hinges to allow for opening and closing the roof.

9 Drill pilot holes and insert two screw eyes on the front panel 3" in from the side panels. Line up the other two screw eyes on the underside of the roof as close to the front screw eyes as possible. Drill pilot holes and insert the screw eyes.

10 Thread wire through each set of eyes and twist tightly to prevent raccoons and other pests from entering the box.

With their favorite habitats—dead trees, snags, and large dead limbs—declining, the strikingly beautiful red-headed woodpecker will find this birdhouse attractive. These woodpeckers also populate open woodlands, farmlands, orchards, and the suburbs where they snare insects in midair and forage on the ground for seeds, worms, mice, spiders, acorns, nuts, and berries. Their houses should be placed 12 to 20 feet off the ground near the edge of the woods. Leave a small pile of wood chips on the floor. This birdhouse also serves the golden-pointed woodpecker.

Materials
1" × 8" × 7' rough-cut cedar
Two hinges and screws
1⅝" rust-resistant screws
Two small 1⅜" screw eyes
Bendable wire

Instructions
❶ Cut pieces from 1"× 8" lumber as follows (pieces except floor and sides are full width of the board):
Back: 20"
Front: 14"
Roof: 8½"
2 sides: 6" × 15"
Floor: 5¾" × 6"

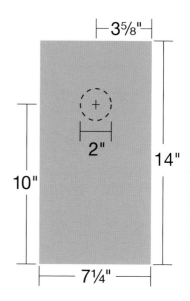

❷ Drill four ¼" drainage holes in the floor.

❸ Mark a point 10" from the bottom of the front panel, centered left and right. Drill a 2" entry hole with the mark at the center of your hole. See the diagram.

❹ On one edge of a side piece measure and mark 1" from the top. Draw a line from the opposite top corner to the 1" mark. Cut on the line at an angle so that the side piece tapers from 15" in the back to 14" in the front. Drill two ¼" ventilation holes at the top of the side panel.

❺ Repeat step 4 with the other side piece.

❻ The back edge of the roof will need to be cut in at the same angle as the side panel to fit flush against the back. Position the back edge of the roof on top of a side piece and trace the angle onto the roof's back edge so that the two pieces form a straight line. Cut the roof at that angle.

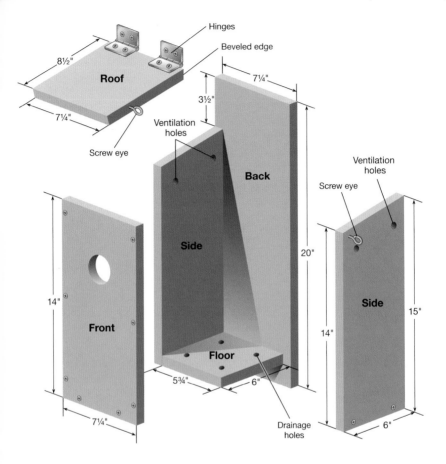

❼ On both edges and the front and back of the back panel, measure 3½" from the top and 1½" from the bottom. Carefully position one side piece against the back with the top edge at the 3½" mark, as shown in the diagram. Drill pilot holes and insert screws to secure the back and side panels.

❽ Position the floor against the back and side panels and flush with the bottom of the side, as shown in the diagram. You should have the mark on the back at 1½" showing you where the bottom of the side ends. Drill pilot holes ⅜" above the mark through the back and into the floor. Secure the floor to the back with screws. Drill pilot holes ⅜" up from the bottom edge of the side piece and secure the floor to the side panel with screws.

⑨ Position the other side panel against the back. Drill pilot holes between the pencil marks on the back and along the bottom edge of the side panel, as in steps 7 and 8. Insert screws to secure this side piece to the back and floor.

⑩ Position the front in place so that the bottom edge is flush with the floor and sides. Drill pilot holes and insert screws to secure.

⑪ Fasten one side of the hinges to the roof with screws. Make sure hinges are oriented so that the roof can lift and close.

⑫ Set the roof in place against the back panel and pivot the other side of the hinge so that it is flat against the back. Mark where holes need to be drilled. Remove the roof and drill pilot holes. Set the roof back in place and insert screws to finish attaching the hinges.

⑬ Drill a hole ¾" in from the front edge of one side panel and ½" down from the top, as shown in the diagram. Insert a screw eye.

⑭ Drill a hole in the edge of the roof to insert the second screw eye above the first one. Thread flexible wire through both to secure the birdhouse.

The elegant tree swallow is a social bird that travels and lives in flocks and favors tree cavities near water such as lakes, streams, woodlands, and marshes. The acrobatic birds snatch flying insects such as dragonflies, grasshoppers, horseflies, and beetles but also feed on seeds and berries. Their nesting box should be mounted 5 to 15 feet high on a tree or post in an open area. The entry hole should face the east. They will construct their nests of grass, twigs, and the feathers of other birds.

Materials

⅜" × 2' × 2' exterior grade plywood
½" × 12" × 12" exterior grade plywood
¼" × 2' × 2' lauan plywood or ¼" × 1½" × 8' pine lattice strips
Water-resistant wood glue
Two 1⅝" rust-resistant screws
Two 1" rust-resistant screws

Exterior-coated nails
Sandpaper
Exterior caulk
Exterior paint in your choice of colors

Instructions

1 Measure and cut from ⅜" plywood:
1 side: 6" × 5⅜"
1 side: 6" × 5"
2 roof pieces: 7" × 7½"

Measure and cut from ½" plywood:
Front: 5" × 5" square
Back: 5" × 5" square
Mounting strip: 2" × 12"

Measure and cut from ¼" lauan:
Shingles for roof: Sixteen 1¼" × 7¾" strips
(Or twelve 7¾" lengths of 1½" pine lattice strips)

2 The 5" squares will be turned to form a diamond shape. Cutting on the diagonal is useful when you need additional strength, but in this case that won't be necessary.

3 On the front diamond panel drill two ¼" ventilation holes in the peak. With your ruler connecting the bottom point and the peak, measure and mark a point 3¾" from the bottom and centered left and right. Drill a 1½" entry hole making the mark the center of the circle.

4 Each roof piece needs to be beveled at a 45-degree angle in order to meet evenly at the peak. Cut each section at that angle. Refer to the diagram to see how they fit together at a 90-degree angle.

Tree Swallow Birdhouse

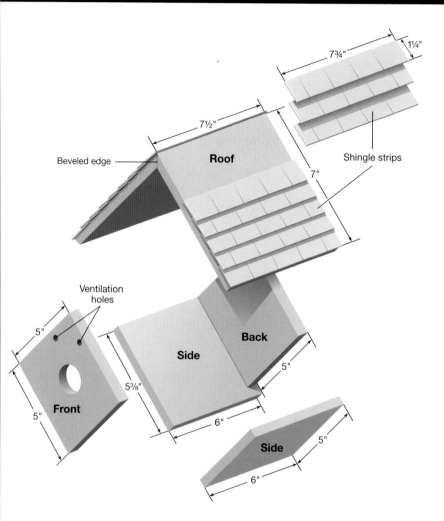

5 Position the lower side of the back diamond flush with the back edge of the 6" × 5⅜" side panel, as shown in the diagram, with ⅜" left open at the bottom. Secure the two sections with nails.

6 Set the front panel in place on the front edge of the 6" × 5⅜" side, so that it's lined up evenly with the back panel, also leaving ⅜" open at the bottom. Secure the lower part of the front panel to the side.

7 Slip the 6" × 5" side section in place on the underside of the house. Drill pilot holes through to the front and back panels and secure it with the 1" screws, which can be removed for cleaning the house.

8 Position one roof section on top of the assembled panels with the back edges flush. Check to make sure both roof pieces will meet tightly at the peak and the roof fits snugly on the birdhouse base. If not, lightly sand any uneven edges. Nail each roof section in place.

9 Take the 1" × 7¾" wood strips and make light saw cuts into their faces in a random manner to give the appearance of wood shingles.

10 Starting at the bottom, attach the strips of wood to the roof with glue, making sure each strip is parallel to the one directly underneath and allowing a small amount of overlap. It might be necessary to use small nails to secure the strips in place. Trim the top strips at the roof peak and apply caulk to seal the seam at the peak.

11 Position the 12" mounting strip on the back of the birdhouse. Drill pilot holes and secure it to the back with 1⅝" screws.

12 Drill two ¼" ventilation holes in the back panel as close to the peak as possible, on either side of the mounting strip.

13 Paint the shingles a gray or brown color to give them a weathered look. Be sure to paint them thoroughly so that water won't penetrate the finish. Paint the rest of the house a color to complement your own home.

The friendly chickadee, which can produce as many as 15 different calls and feed upside down, nests in tree cavities, old fence posts, and nest boxes such as this one. They frequent city and country landscapes where there are trees and underbrush. Their diet consists of insects they pick from tree crevices, as well as berries, tiny seeds, and suet. The chickadee birdhouse should be mounted on a tree, pole, or fence post about 4 to 12 feet above the ground.

Materials

½" × 2' × 2' exterior grade plywood
1½" rust-resistant screws
Gray paint
Fine grade sandpaper

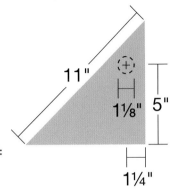

Instructions

1 Measure and cut the following
from a 2' square sheet of plywood:
Back: 6" × 16"
Roof: 5½" × 9½"
Sides: Two 7¾" × 7¾" × 11"
    triangles
Base: 5" × 8¼"

2 To make two triangular side panels, first cut a 7¾" × 7¾" square
from the plywood sheet. Draw a diagonal line through the center
that connects two opposite corners of the square. Cut on that line
to make the two triangles.

3 Where the roof meets the back it needs to be bevel-cut back from
9½" on the top side to 9" on the bottom of the roof, as shown in
the diagram. Measure and bevel the edge.

4 One end of the base will also need to be cut at an angle to fit flush
against the back. The bottom face of the base is 8¼" long and the
inside face that is attached to the sides is 7¾" long. Measure and
bevel-cut the end.

5 On one side panel, lay out the center point of the entry hole,
using the diagram shown above. Drill a 1⅛" diameter entry hole
with your mark at the center of the circle.

6 Drill two ¼" ventilation holes in the other side as shown in the
diagram.

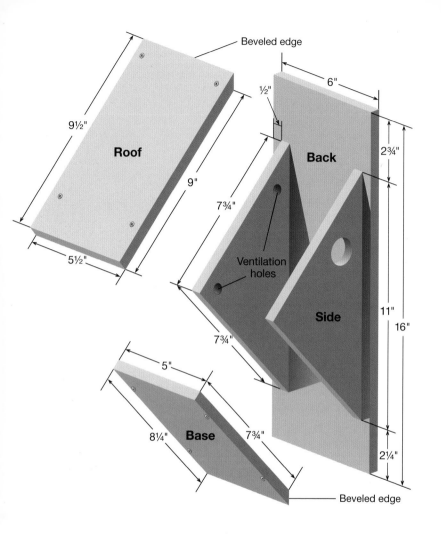

Beveled edge

Roof

9½"

9"

7¾"

5½"

½"

6"

Back

2¾"

7¾"

Ventilation
holes

Side

11"

16"

5"

8¼"

Base

7¾"

7¾"

2¼"

Beveled edge

7 Use the diagram shown above to lay out the positions of both side panels on the back panel. Draw layout lines on the back face of the back panel to locate installation screws for the sides that are centered on the thicknesses of these panels. Drill pilot holes and insert screws. Make sure the entry hole is oriented toward the roof, not the base.

⑧ Position the base in place with the beveled end against the back panel. Drill pilot holes and secure with screws.

⑨ Set the roof in place on top. It should be slightly wider than the house, so be sure it is centered, and take that into account when drilling pilot holes, which should be about ½" in from each long edge of the roof. Secure the roof to the sides with screws.

⑩ Paint the outside of the house gray. After it is dry, lightly sand it to give it a more weathered look.

Barn Owl Nesting Box

The barn owl, whose population has been on the decline, nests in hollow trees, barns, and buildings, but this nesting box placed within a mile of their hunting grounds can aid in restoring the species. They feed on mice and other small rodents that inhabit short grasses in dairy pastureland, wet meadows, and marshes. The box entrance should be 20 to 25 feet above the ground and mounted against the inside wall of a barn or building. A 6" to 6 ½" hole can be cut through the wall so they can enter from the outside. If so, the entrance flight path should be clear and face toward the grasslands where the owls hunt.

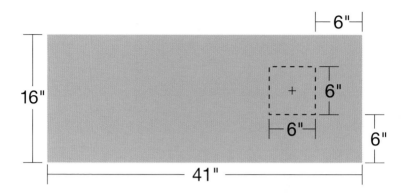

Materials

$\frac{1}{2}$" × 4' × 8' plywood

$1\frac{5}{8}$" rust-resistant screws

Two hinges

Safety hasp

Large screw eyes and about 6' of bendable wire

Instructions

If you are mounting the box against a barn wall with the entrance on the outside, there will be no front for the box because the inside wall of the barn will act as its front. These are the instructions for when that isn't feasible.

❶ Measure and cut the following pieces from the plywood:

Bottom: 12" × 42"

Front: 16" × 41"

Back: 16" × 41"

Top: 12" × 42"

2 sides: 12" × 16"

❷ On the front panel measure and mark a 6" square as shown on the diagram. Cut out the square to form the entrance hole.

Barn Owl Nesting Box

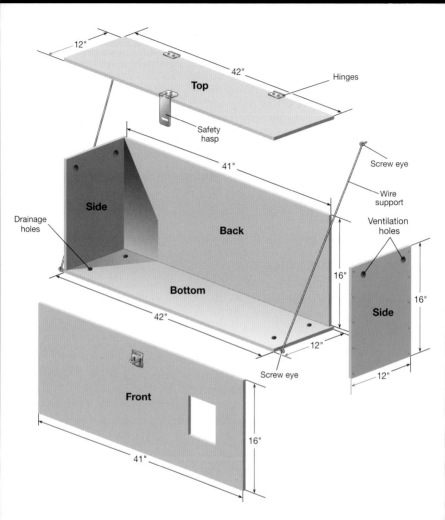

3 Drill two ¾" ventilation holes in each side piece as shown in the diagram. Drill four ¾" drainage holes in the floor.

4 The back sits between the two side panels. Position one side piece beside the back. Drill pilot holes through the side panel and install screws to secure the side to the back panel. Attach the other side in a similar manner.

5 Set the bottom panel in place against the sides and back. Drill pilot holes through it and secure the bottom with screws.

6 Set the front in place between the two side panels. Drill pilot holes and secure it with screws.

7 Set the top in place. Mark where the hinges need pilot holes drilled. Drill the holes and attach the hinges to the top and back sections so the lid can open and close for cleaning.

8 Position the safety hasp so that it will latch on the top and front of the nesting box, and mark where the screws will be inserted. Drill pilot holes and attach the hasp. Secure the hasp with wire that can be twisted easily.

9 One way to mount this large box is to fasten a long cleat to the bottom panel and drive screws through the cleat into wall studs. Support the front of the house with long wire tied to screw eyes in the wall and box. Drill pilot holes both in the wall and the front side of the box. Insert the screw eyes and wire as shown in the diagram.

Building a log feeder is relatively easy and can be done with natural material, either a tree trunk or new-fallen tree branch. White birch, pine, or ash are good choices. You have lots of options, such as the type of tree, how long and how thick the log will be, and the number of perches you wish to have. Or you may decide to have no perches at all, making it more attractive to such birds as nuthatches and wood-peckers whose toes cling well to tree bark.

Materials

14"–16" log, 4"–6" in diameter
$\frac{1}{4}$" diameter dowel 1' long
Wood glue
One $1\frac{5}{8}$" screw eye
12"–18" of flexible wire for hanging

Instructions

1 Measure down 3" from the top of the log and mark a point. Mark another point 6" below the first.

2 Using a drill, make 1½" diameter holes on the marks about ¾" to 1" deep, with the mark at the center of the hole.

3 Turn the log a quarter turn. Measure and mark a point 4½" from the top. Mark another point 6 inches below the first. Drill 1½" holes on these marks, as in step 2.

4 Rotate the log a quarter turn and repeat steps 1 and 2 with measurements and holes at 3" and 9".

5 Rotate the log a quarter turn and repeat step 2 with measurements and holes at 4½" and 10½".

6 Drill ¼" diameter holes about 1" deep, ½" below 4 of the large holes.

7 Cut four 2½" lengths from the dowel.

8 Glue the dowel pieces into the holes, leaving the exposed parts as perches.

9 Mark a point on top of the log in the center. Drill a pilot hole and insert the screw eye.

10 Insert one end of the flexible wire through the screw eye and twist tightly. Hang from a tree limb.

11 Mix bird seed in peanut butter and fill the holes with the mixture for tasty treats for your birds.

This is a very basic but attractive bird feeder. Once you've got it constructed, fill 'er up with different varieties of seeds from week to week to see which species enjoy which seeds.

Materials

½" × 12" × 12" exterior grade plywood
1" × 2" × 2' cedar or pine
¼" × 2½" dowel
8" × 7½" piece of window screen
1" × 2" × 5' post
Rust-resistant screws and finishing nails
Staples
Water-resistant wood glue

Instructions

1 From the plywood cut the following pieces:
Back: 8" × 12"
Roof: Two 2" × 5½" lengths

2 From the 1" × 2" cedar or pine cut the following pieces:
Sides: Two 6" lengths
Front: One 8" length

3 Measure and mark the center of the top edge of the back panel at 4". Measure and mark a point on one edge of the back 2" from the top. With a pencil and ruler lightly trace a line from the center point to the mark on the edge.

4 Repeat your measurement with the other edge as in step 3.

5 Cut along the pencil lines to create a peaked roof.

6 Measure and mark a point 5" from the top and centered left and right. Drill a 1¼" diameter hole with the mark at the center of the hole.

7 ¾" below the hole above, drill a ¼" hole, centered.

8 Position a side piece in front of the back, with the bottom edges flush and even. Drill a pilot hole in the back panel and attach the side piece with a screw.

Bird-Feeding Stations

Instead of one bird feeder in the backyard, you may consider a bird-feeding station. That means putting up three or four or more feeders at different heights and with a variety of food, thus attracting a wider variety of birds.

Location is key. The feeders should be in a clear area where you can see the birds, and you will want shrubs and trees to be close enough that the birds can take cover from predators.

Most birds dine at one or more different areas. The four main categories are ground level, table top, hanging, and tree trunk.

Juncos, sparrows, towhees, and mourning doves are among those that eat at ground level, and wooden platform feeders just above the ground line are perfect.

Wrens, chickadees, blue jays, cardinals, grosbeaks, and titmice enjoy feasting on table tops. These might be windowsills, a deck railing, or a picnic table. So windowsill feeders are just the ticket, as are those designed to go on deck railings.

Hanging feeders appeal to nuthatches, chickadees, titmice, and finches. Cylindrical-style hanging feeders containing Nyjer and sunflower seeds fit the bill.

Finally, suet feeders against tree trunks are magnets for a variety of woodpeckers, chickadees, jays, brown creepers, and titmice.

9 Attach the second side piece as in step 8.

10 Position the front panel in front of the two side pieces. Secure it with finishing nails.

11 Position the 8" × 7½" screen on the underside of the feeding tray. Use a staple gun to attach the screen to the bottom of the tray and the back of the panel. Trim to fit.

12 Using wood glue, secure the dowel in the ¼" hole.

13 The ends of the roof pieces that meet at the peak will need to be cut at an angle so that they meet evenly. (See the diagram for the Prairie Feeder.) Bevel-cut one end of both sections at a 30-degree angle.

14 Position the roof sections on top of the back panel with the beveled ends held together. Mark a line on the outer end of each roof section that makes the edge parallel to the sides of the back panel. Cut the edges off.

15 Set one side of the roof in place with the overhang extending over the feeder tray. Secure it to the back with finishing nails.

16 Set the second side of the roof in place and secure it as in step 15.

17 Paint a fence around the feeder tray and decorate your Down Home Bird Feeder to suit your taste.

18 Taper the end of the post into a point so that it can be driven into the ground.

19 Drill two pilot holes into one of the faces of the post near the top. Attach the back of the feeder to the post with screws.

Here is a bird feeding station that is a bit different from most, but it can really satisfy a lot of hungry birds at the same time. While it may seem complicated to build, it is not really that difficult. It needs to be mounted against a post on your deck or a flat surface such as a fence post.

Materials

1" × 6" × 10' pine
2" × 6" × 2' pine
1⅝" screws
1½" brass hinge with
    screws
Silicone cement
Exterior paint or sealer

Instructions

❶ From the 1" × 6" × 10' measure and cut the following:
2 sides: 5½" × 24"
Front: 4" × 24"
Back: 4" × 24"
5 roof pieces: 3½" × 2¼"
5 roof pieces: 2¾" × 2¼"

From the 2" × 6" × 2' measure and cut the following:
Lid piece: 5½" × 5½"
Feeder board: 4" × 4"
Three feeder base boards: 4" × 3"
Base for mounting: 5½" × 7"

❷ Take the 4" feeder board and bevel-cut it twice so that there is a 1½" peak at the center beveling to ½" thickness at the edges, creating a slope that will help direct seeds toward the lowest holes. See diagram on page 62.

❸ On each of the 5½" × 24" side pieces, measure and mark a point 8½" from the top and another point 11½" below the first one. Center both points. Drill 1" feed holes in the two side pieces where marked, with your mark at the center of the hole.

❹ On the 4" × 24" front piece, measure a point 13" from the top and centered left and right. Drill a 1" feed hole, with the mark at the center of the hole. Note: the back piece will have no holes.

❺ In the center of each 4" × 3" feeder base, drill a 1" diameter hole 1" deep. Split these workpieces through the center to create five base boards plus one extra.

❻ On the back side of the 24" boards, hold a feeder base at the midpoint of each hole. Lightly trace around each base to give you the area to position your screws.

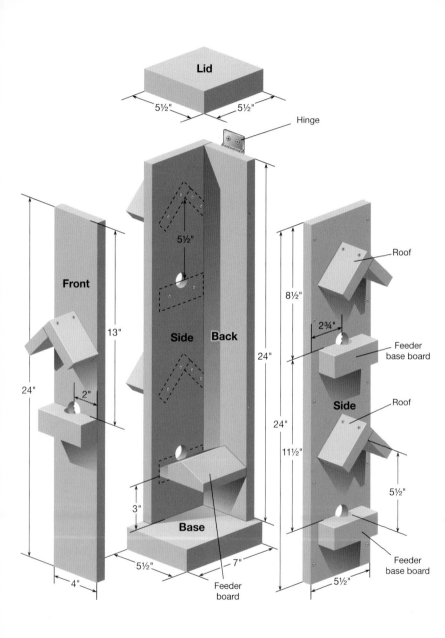

Lid

5½" 5½"

Hinge

Front

24"

13"

2"

5½"

Side Back

24"

24"

11½"

8½"

2¾"

Roof

Feeder base board

Side

Roof

5½"

Feeder base board

3"

Base

5½" 7"

Feeder board

4"

5½"

7 Measure 5½" up from the top of each tracing and carefully position 2 roof pieces to form a roof peak similar to the diagram on the next page, with the longer edge overlapping the shorter one. Trace around the outer edges of the roof.

8 Repeat step 7 for the other 4 holes.

9 Place each feeder base in the correct position on the outside of the 24" boards. The top ½" of the feeding hole is exposed and the bottom ½" of the feeding hole feeds into the semicircle of the feeder base, as shown in the diagram.

10 Drill pilot holes inside the tracing outlines made in step 6 and secure each base with 1⅝" screws.

11 Position each section of the roof in place 5½" above the feeder base, as shown in the diagram. Drill pilot holes inside the tracing made in step 7. Secure each roof piece with 1⅝" screws. Repeat the process with the other 4 roofs.

12 To assemble the feeder, position one side panel beside the back panel with the side edge even with the back, as shown in the diagram. Drill pilot holes through the side and into the back and insert screws. Repeat this process with the other side panel.

13 Position the feeder board made in step 2 between the sides and against the back panel as shown in the diagram. The beveled edge should be just under the feeder hole drilled on each side panel, and the base of the feeder board should be 3" above the feeder bottom. Drill pilot holes from the back to secure it from that side. You will also need to secure it through the front panel after the front has been set in place.

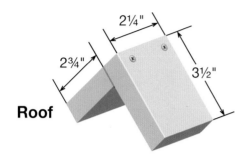

Roof

$2\frac{3}{4}$"

$2\frac{1}{4}$"

$3\frac{1}{2}$"

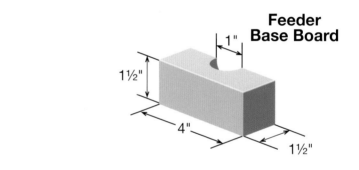

Feeder Base Board

1"

$1\frac{1}{2}$"

4"

$1\frac{1}{2}$"

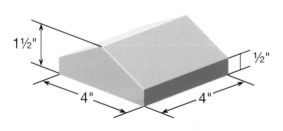

$1\frac{1}{2}$"

$\frac{1}{2}$"

4"

4"

Feeder Board

⑭ Position the front panel between the two sides. Drill pilot holes and secure the front with screws.

⑮ The 5½" lid will be attached to the feeder with the 1½" hinge. Position the hinge in place centered on the back of the lid. Mark where the pilot holes will be drilled. Drill pilot holes and secure the top half of the hinge to the lid with screws.

⑯ Attach the other side of the hinge to the back of the feeder with screws. Set the lid in place on the feeder.

⑰ Position the feeder on top of the base so that the pieces are flush in the back and the single feeder hole is facing the front. Turn the base over and drill pilot holes ⅜" from the edge along the sides and back. Measure and mark a point 5" from the back of the base. Drill pilot holes across the base at this layout line to secure the base to the feeder with screws.

⑱ Seal the feeder with exterior sealer or paint and decorate your feeder. Then mount it against any flat surface, such as a fence post or a deck railing.

There are a wide a variety of suet feeders just as there are plenty of varieties of suet bird food cakes, but all will appeal to such wild birds as woodpeckers, bluebirds, wrens, and cardinals. The cakes of saturated fats may also include insects, birdseeds, raisins, or nuts as ingredients. The birds especially go for the suet in the springtime after flying long distances from their winter homes.

Materials

¼" or ½" galvanized or plastic hardware cloth for netting,
    cut to 9" × 4¾"
½" exterior grade plywood 2' × 2'
Two small hinges and screws
1½" rust-resistant screws
Staples
Duct tape
Two small screw eyes and bendable wire (optional)

Instructions

1 Measure and cut the plywood to the following dimensions:
    Bottom: 6" × 2½"
    Back: 6" × 6¾"
    2 sides: 2" × 7¼"
    Roof: 3" × 8"
    Mounting strips: ½" × 6" and 2" × 10"

2 Take a 2" × 7¼" side piece and measure and mark a point 2"
    down from the top of one edge. With a pencil and ruler draw a
    line from the opposite top edge to the 2" mark. Cut on the line so
    that your side piece now tapers from 7¼" on one edge to 5¼" on
    the other. This shorter edge will face the front, and the 7¼" edge
    will be attached to the back panel.

3 Repeat step 2 with the other side piece.

4 Hold a side panel in place beside the back piece with their top
    edges together. Mark the angle of the side piece on the back
    panel. The top of the back edge will need to be bevel-cut toward
    the front, so that it matches the angle of the side piece. Also
    bevel-cut the back edge of the roof so that it can fit flat against the
    mounting strip.

⑤ Position the back in place on top of the bottom panel. Drill pilot holes up through the bottom and secure it to the back with screws.

⑥ If using galvanized hardware cloth, the netting edge may be sharp. For protection, measure a 1" × 8" piece of duct tape and fold it over the top. Cut two 1" × 4 ¾" pieces for the sides.

⑦ Position the netting even with the top of the left side of the feeder with 1½" extending into the inside. Staple it in place as close to the front edge as possible. Bend it at a 90-degree angle.

⑧ Bend the other edge of netting at a 90-degree angle and staple it in place on the inside of the right side of the feeder as in step 7. There should be 6" of netting in the middle left unattached.

⑨ Position the left side beside the bottom and flush with the back of the feeder so that the 5¼" edge is facing forward. Drill pilot holes and secure the side to the back and bottom with screws.

⑩ Position the right side of the feeder against the back and bottom as in step 9, with the netting in the front. Drill pilot holes and attach the right side to the back and bottom with screws.

⑪ Set the ½" × 6" mounting strip on the inside of the netting, at its top edge between the side panels. Drill pilot holes through the sides and secure the mounting strip with screws.

⑫ The roof of the feeder will flip down from the front. Position one side of the hinge on the inside of the mounting strip. Mark where the pilot holes will be drilled. Drill holes and insert the screws.

⑬ Position the roof in place, with the back of the roof even with the back of the feeder. Position the other half of the hinge on the underside of the roof at the front. Mark where pilot holes will be drilled, and secure the hinge with screws.

⑭ If you want to hang the feeder, insert screw eyes on the sides of the feeder just below the roof. Thread bendable wire through the screw eyes and twist tightly to make a hanger. To mount the feeder to a wall, center the 10" mounting strip on the back panel and secure it with screws. Fill your feeder with suet and invite your bird friends in for a tasty and nutritious treat.

The base of this feeder is a buffet-style tray that can be left open to the elements, but adding the canopy provides some measure of shelter for the seeds. Meanwhile, the dining birds stay high and dry.

Materials

¾" × 12" × 12" exterior grade plywood
1" × 2" × 4' pine or cedar
12" or 14" × 24" rolled aluminum
Eight ½" screws
Rust-resistant nails

Instructions

1 Measure and cut from ¾" plywood:
Base: 9" × 10½"

Measure and cut from pine or cedar:
2 sides: 9" long
2 sides: 12" long

Measure and cut from aluminum:
Canopy: 12" × 24"

2 Drill four ¼" holes in the plywood for drainage.

3 Position one 9" side piece against one short end of the plywood. It should be flush with the bottom of the plywood. Nail it in place.

4 Repeat step 3 with the other short end.

5 Set one long side piece in place against one of the longer sides of the feeder. The longer piece will overlap the shorter sides. Nail it to the plywood and into the ends of the shorter strips, securing the corners.

6 Repeat step 5 with the other long side.

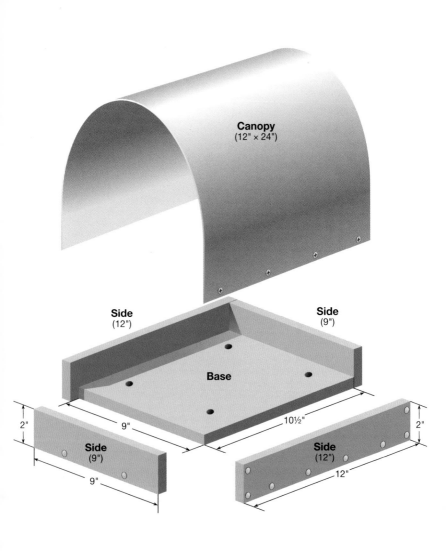

Canopy
(12" × 24")

Side
(12")

Side
(9")

Base

Side
(9")

Side
(12")

2"

9"

10½"

9"

2"

12"

7 Drill four evenly spaced holes through each of the 12" ends of the aluminum.

8 Position one drilled end of the aluminum in place against the longer side of the feeder tray. Drill four pilot holes into the wood, through the holes made in the aluminum, and insert four screws.

9 Position the other end of the aluminum against the opposite long side, forming a canopy for your feeder. Drill four pilot holes into the wood and insert four screws.

10 Attach the feeder to the top of a post.

A touch of gray paint and a bit of sandpaper give this plywood feeder a nostalgic effect, but for the birds it will serve as a brand-new restaurant.

Materials

½" × 2' × 2' exterior grade plywood
8" × 7" piece of ¼"or ½" galvanized or plastic hardware cloth
Exterior-coated nails
Staples

Two ¾" × ¾" rust-resistant hinges with screws
Gray paint
Sandpaper

Instructions

1. Measure and cut the following from ½" plywood:
   Base: 10" × 9"
   Back: 5" × 7"
   2 sides: 5" × 9½"
   Roof piece: 8½" × 5"
   Roof piece: 8½" × 5½"

2. On one of the two sides, measure and mark a point on one edge 7" from the bottom. Repeat with the other edge. On the top end, locate and mark the panel's centerpoint. Draw a straight line that connects the 7" mark on the edge to the top center mark. Repeat with the other edge to the top center mark. Cut on both lines to create the peak on the side of the feeder.

3. Repeat step 2 to measure and cut the other side piece like the first one.

4. Position the left side panel so its back edge is flush with the back face of the back panel. Nail the side to the edge of the back panel.

5. Hold the hardware cloth so that you are working with the 7" high edges. Bend 1½" of both edges of the hardware cloth at 90-degree angles. Make sure the edges are facing the same direction. You should have a 5" section of netting between the two bends. Position one edge at the front of the left side on the inside. Staple the netting in place as close as possible to the front edge.

6. Position the unattached edge of the netting on the inside of the right side with 1½" overlapping the inside face. Staple the hardware cloth on the inside as close to the front as possible. There

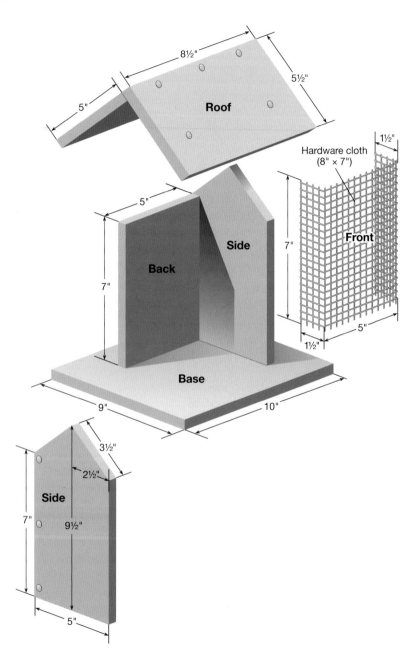

8½"

5½"

5"

Roof

Hardware cloth
(8" × 7")

1½"

7"

Front

5"

1½"

5"

Side

Back

7"

Base

9"

10"

3½"

2½"

Side

7"

9½"

5"

should be a 5" section of unattached netting that will serve as the front of the feeder.

7 Position the right side of the feeder in place beside the back. Nail the side to the edge of the back panel.

8 Position the 5½" × 8½" roof panel over the front section with ½" extending past the peak, as shown in the diagram. Center it over the sides with an overhang on either side and extending over the front netting. Nail it in place to the sides.

9 Position the other roof panel in place under the ½" overhang at the peak so that it is flush with the ends of the first roof section already installed.

10 Set one side of the hinges in place at the top of the 5" roof panel. Mark where to drill pilot holes. Secure the hinge with screws.

11 Repeat step 10 to install the other side of the hinge to the other roof section.

12 Paint the feeder and allow it to dry.

13 Sand the feeder lightly with the sandpaper to give it an aged, weathered effect.

14 Center the feeder on the 10" wide by 9" deep base with 2" of edge showing all around. Measure in 2¼" from each edge of the base on the underside and drive nails through the base into the back and side panels.

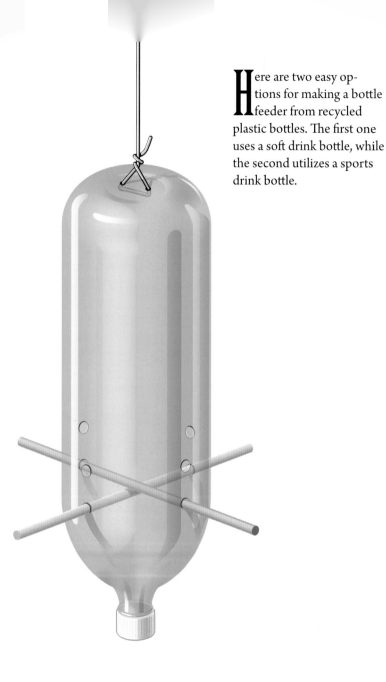

ere are two easy options for making a bottle feeder from recycled plastic bottles. The first one uses a soft drink bottle, while the second utilizes a sports drink bottle.

Bottle Feeder No. 1

Materials
2-liter plastic soft drink bottle
$\frac{1}{4}$" dowel rod 36" long (to be used for both projects)
36" thick florists' wire
Exterior caulk or duct tape

Instructions

1 Cut two 8½" pieces from the dowel rod.

2 Wash and clean the bottle in hot water. Fill the bottle with hot tap water and allow it to soak in order to loosen the glue on the base.

3 Remove the base piece and the label from the bottle.

4 Drill two ⅛" holes about 1½" apart through the bottom of the bottle. With the cap off, feed the wire through one of the ⅛" holes all the way to the mouth of the bottle, while holding onto the other end. Twist the wire around and thread it back up through the other ⅛" hole. Twist the wire to form a loop for your hanger. Trim off the excess. Use caulk or duct tape to seal the holes to keep your seeds dry.

5 Drill two ¼" holes opposite each other about 4" from the top of the bottle. Poke an 8½" long dowel rod through the first set of holes. Rotate the bottle a quarter turn and drill the second set of holes ¾" below the first set. Poke the other dowel rod through these holes for your second set of perches.

6 Size the openings for bird seed based on the type of seed you will use. With a razor blade cut four ¼" by ⅜" slots about 1½" above each of the perches for Nyjer (thistle) seeds. Drill or cut ⁵⁄₁₆" round openings for black oil sunflower seeds.

7 You'll need a funnel to fill your 2-liter bottle with seeds, but it will hold a lot more treats for your feathered friends than the smaller feeder.

Bottle Feeder No. 2

Materials
32-ounce sports drink plastic bottle
¼" dowel rod 36" long (to be used for both projects)
24" thick florists' wire
Exterior caulk

Instructions

1 Cut a 7" length from the dowel rod.

2 Remove the label from the bottle and wash the bottle thoroughly.

3 Drill two ⅛" holes in the bottom of the bottle about 1" to 1½" apart. Thread the stiff florists' wire through the holes and twist it to form a loop for attaching your hanger.

4 After the wire has been threaded, seal around the holes with caulk to keep the seeds dry.

5 Drill two ¼" holes opposite each other about 2" from the top of the bottle. Poke a 6" dowel through one hole and out the other to form two perches.

6 Make openings for the bird seed as in the instructions for the other bottle, step 6.

7 Fill the bottle with seeds, screw on the bottle top, and find a place to hang your feeder.

This feeder is shaped and painted like a barn. The acrylic roof allows you to check out which birds are having a hoedown as they feast in the country-style feeder.

Materials

¾" × 2' × 2' exterior grade plywood
1⅝" rust-resistant screws
Finishing nails
Two 1⅜" screw eyes
Barn red, white, and black acrylic paint and small paint brush

8" × 10" acrylic sheet, .08" thick
⅝" rust-resistant screws (for roof)
X-ACTO knife and blades
Wire or cord for hanging
Wood filler and sandpaper

Instructions

❶ Measure and cut the following from a 2' square sheet of plywood:
2 end panels: 7" × 8½"
Bottom: 9" × 7"
Top: 9" × 2"
2 side pieces: 7½" × 2"

❷ You will also need to measure and cut two 9" × 4" pieces from the acrylic sheet for the roof. After marking your measurements on the sheet, hold a ruler on the measurement line at an angle and score or scribe the acrylic with an X-ACTO blade or other sharp knife. You may need to do this more than once. Then position the scored line on the edge of a flat surface like a countertop with the ruler flat against the counter at the line. Apply pressure on top of the ruler and snap the acrylic down along the cut.

❸ Take an end panel and measure and mark 6" from the bottom on both edges. Then along the top edge, mark a point at 2½" in from each side edge. Draw a line from each edge mark at 6" to the top mark closest to that edge. Cut along each line.

❹ Trace the measurements for the barn door before you begin assembly. On the bottom edge, measure 2" from each side and mark those points. With a pencil make a 5¾" high and 3" wide rectangle using the 2" measurements as a guide, as shown in the diagram. Make another rectangle ½" inside the outer one. Starting at the top, measure 2⅛" down from the inside rectangle toward the center. Do this from both sides and draw a line to complete the top box for your "X" mark. Repeat this process from the bottom,

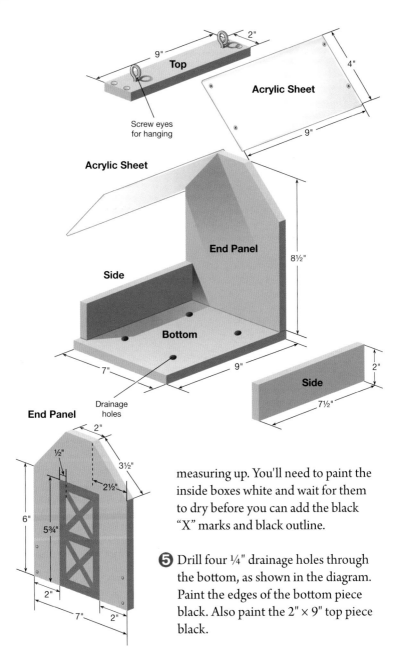

Top

9"

2"

Acrylic Sheet

4"

9"

Screw eyes
for hanging

Acrylic Sheet

End Panel

8½"

Side

Bottom

7"

9"

2"

Side

7½"

Drainage
holes

End Panel

2"

½"

3½"

2½"

6"

5¾"

2"

7"

2"

measuring up. You'll need to paint the
inside boxes white and wait for them
to dry before you can add the black
"X" marks and black outline.

❺ Drill four ¼" drainage holes through
the bottom, as shown in the diagram.
Paint the edges of the bottom piece
black. Also paint the 2" × 9" top piece
black.

⑥ To assemble the feeder, start with an end panel and set it on the bottom with the 7" ends together. From the underside, drill pilot holes and secure the end panel with screws. Repeat with the other end panel.

⑦ Set a 7½" long side piece between the end panels and nail them together at the outer edges. From the underside, drill pilot holes and secure the bottom to the side pieces with screws.

⑧ Position the black top piece on top of the end panels. After drilling countersunk pilot holes, insert screws to secure the top to the sides. Fill the screwholes with wood filler and touch them up with black paint.

⑨ Recess the nailheads on the end panels and fill the holes with wood filler. Sand to a smooth finish. Paint the barn red.

⑩ Position one side of the acrylic roof in place. Drill pilot holes and secure the roof with ⅝" screws. Be careful not to overtighten them.

⑪ Drill pilot holes in the top piece and insert the two screw eyes for hanging your feeder with wire or cord.

This Snack Bar Feeder is a simple project, and a good one to use as a teaching lesson for children. You may be able to use wood scraps rather than cedar, and it allows you to recycle a plastic bottle as the seed container.

Materials

1" × 6" × 3' cedar

1½" rust-resistant screws

Two small 1" screw eyes

8"-tall 32-ounce sports drink bottle, washed and dried

18" string or twine

Instructions

1 Measure and cut the following pieces from the 1" × 6" lumber (all pieces will be the full width of the board):

Back: 11"

Base: 7"

Top: 6¼"

Support piece: 2¾"

❷ Measure and mark a point 2¼" in from the front edge of the base, centered from left to right. Using a spade bit, drill a 2½" diameter hole about ⅜" deep in the base, using your mark as the center of the circle.

❸ Position the back on top of the base. Drill pilot holes through the base and into the back panel. Insert screws to secure the back.

❹ Position the top piece in front of the back panel. Drill pilot holes from the back into the top panel and insert screws.

❺ Measure the diameter of the base of the plastic bottle, which should be its widest point. The bottle used was 3¾" wide. Cut a semi-circle in the front of the support piece with a diameter of 4". You can adjust your dimensions if you use a bottle wider than 4".

❻ Mark the center of the support piece at 2¾" and the outside edge of your semi-circle at 2" from the centered mark. Make your cut.

❼ Position the support piece against the back panel with the opening facing forward about 4¼" above the base. Drill pilot holes in the back 5" from the bottom edge and insert screws to secure the support piece.

❽ Drill pilot holes on the edges of the front support about 2" from the back panel. Install the screw eyes.

❾ Fill the bottle with bird seed and turn it upside down on the feeder. Secure the bottle with twine or string wrapped around the bottle and each end tied to a screw eye. Set the feeder on the front porch or other handy spot where it can easily be refilled.

This feeder takes more work to construct, but when you're done you will have a miniature grain elevator similar to those which populate the Great Plains, and the birds will be flocking to it. You can also personalize this project by naming the mock grain elevator after your own family. It would be easy to make this feeder into a birdhouse by omitting the feeder features and drilling an entrance hole in the front panel.

Materials

1" × 6" × 8' pine lumber or cedar
¼" × 2' × 2' lauan plywood
¾" × 12" × 12" exterior grade
    plywood for base
1⅝" rust-resistant screws
1 small screw for the back cover
Finishing nails and wood filler
Small nails for the roofs
Water-resistant wood glue
Sandpaper
Exterior paint

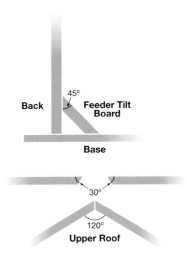

Back   45°   Feeder Tilt
                     Board

Base

30°

120°
Upper Roof

Instructions

1 Measure and cut the following from the pine or cedar lumber:
Front: 5½" × 11"
Back: 5½" × 11"
2 lower sides: 4" × 6¾"
2 upper sides: 4" × 2¼"
2 porch supports: 2" × 4"
Feeder tilt board: 4" × 3¾"

Measure and cut from the lauan plywood:
2 lower roofs: 6" × 1⅞"
2 upper roofs: 6" × 2⅜"
Porch roof: 5" × 2⅝"
Back cover: 2¼" diameter circle

2 Measure and cut a 9½" × 11½" piece from the ¾" plywood for a base.

3 Measure and mark the pattern on the 5½" × 11" front panel as follows: Find the 2¾" midpoint at the bottom and top of the wood and mark them. Mark the following measurements from the bottom on both sides of the front panel: 6¾"; 7¾"; 10". Hold a ruler parallel to the longer side and 1¼" in from the edge. Draw a straight line that is parallel to the edge from the 7¾"mark to the 10" mark. Repeat with the other side.

❸ Draw a straight line on an angle to connect the 10" mark on the inner line to the midpoint mark at the top center. Repeat with the other side. This forms the peak of the feeder roof.

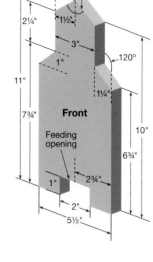

❹ The lower roof line is formed by connecting the measurement mark on the outer edge at 6¾" to the bottom of the inner line which started at 7¾". Repeat with the other side. Make sure your lines are evenly drawn and one side is a mirror image of the other. When you are sure your measurements are accurate, cut out the front panel.

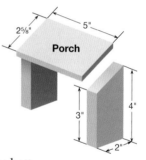

❺ The opening for dispensing the seeds is made in the front section, centered at the bottom. Measure 1" on both sides of the center mark you made. Draw lines 1" up from those marks and connect the parallel lines at the top to make a rectangle. Carefully cut out the opening.

❻ The back of the feeder can be measured by tracing the front outline onto the back piece and cutting on the lines; but there will be a circular opening cut in the back for filling the feeder instead of using the front opening. Measure and mark a point in the back panel centered from left to right and 5" up from the bottom. With a spade bit, drill a 1½" diameter circle with the mark at the center of the

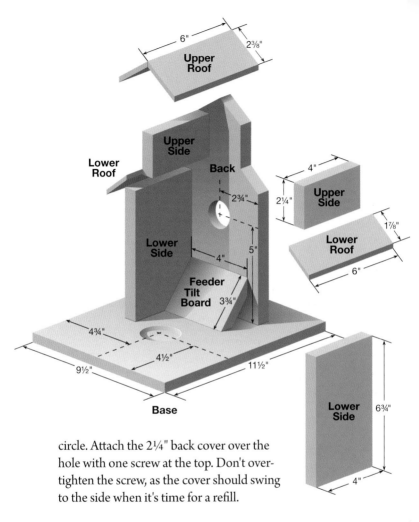

Upper Roof

6"

2⅜"

Lower Roof

Upper Side

Back

Upper Side

4"

2¾"

2¼"

Lower Roof

1⅞"

6"

Lower Side

4"

5"

Feeder Tilt Board

3¾"

Base

4¾"

4½"

9½"

11½"

Lower Side

6¾"

4"

circle. Attach the 2¼" back cover over the hole with one screw at the top. Don't over-tighten the screw, as the cover should swing to the side when it's time for a refill.

7 A tilt board will be inserted against the back panel to help move the seed toward the front of the feeder. The tilt board will be 4" wide and 3¾" long. You will need to bevel-cut the top edge at a 45-degree angle so that it will fit flush against the back panel. It will also need to be bevel-cut at a 45-degree angle where it meets the base. See the diagram for details. Hold the board against the back so that you can see how the cut needs to be made. Do the same for the bottom edge.

8 Each porch support needs to be cut from 4" where it meets the front panel, to 3" at the front. Measure and mark a point 1" down from the top edge of one side. Draw a line to connect the 4" back corner to the 1" measurement and cut on that line. Repeat with the other porch support.

9 Position a porch support ⅜" from the side of the front panel, making sure the bottom edges are even and the longer edge is against the front section. Drill pilot holes from the back and secure the support with screws. Repeat with the other support.

10 The leading edge of the porch roof needs to be cut back at a 30-degree angle in order to fit flush against the front panel. Measure and cut the angle and square off the front edge at the overhang as shown in the diagram. Glue the roof to the front panel and nail it to the supports.

11 Position one 4" × 6¾" lower side section in front of the back panel. The top of this section should be even with where the lower roof line cuts in toward the center of the back. Secure the side to the back with nails. Repeat with the other lower side section.

12 Position the tilt board between the side sections so that the top edge is flush against the back. It should fit tightly but can be secured with nails if needed.

13 Position the front panel on top of the sides and nail them together with finishing nails.

14 Position the upper side panels in place above the lower roof line. Secure them to the feeder with nails.

15 The leading edge of each 2⅜" top roof piece needs to be bevel-cut to a 30-degree angle in order to meet evenly at the peak. See the diagram. Cut one roof section and then cut the other with a reverse angle. Square off the lower edge so that it will be parallel to the feeder. Glue the two roof sections together and glue them in place at the top. When the glue is dry, secure the roof with nails.

⑯ You will need to cut each section of the lower roof at a 30-degree angle where it meets the wood on the top. Repeat the procedure in step 15 to cut and install each of the lower roof sections.

⑰ Recess the nail heads in the panels and those attaching the roof sections. Fill them with wood filler. When dry, sand them to create a flat surface.

⑱ Paint the roof sections and the back cover. Also paint the feeder if you used pine lumber, before attaching it to the base. When it's dry you can stencil and paint your family name on the front panel in another color.

⑲ On the 9½"-wide side of the base, mark a center point. Measure in from the center 4½" and mark that point. Drill a 2" diameter circle about ⅜" deep with the mark at the center of the circle.

⑳ Position the feeder on top of the base with 2" in the back and 2"on either side. The cut-out circle under the front porch is a feeding trough for your backyard birds.

㉑ On the bottom face of the base measure 2½" in from the back and side edges. Drill pilot holes and secure the feeder to the base with screws. Measure in from the front 4⅜". Drill pilot holes and secure the front corners with screws.

㉒ When filling the feeder, use masking tape to cover the opening to prevent seeds from spilling out. After it's filled, peel it off and you're ready to go.

Black oil sunflower seed is the most universally eaten food eaten at bird feeders. But there are many types of seeds, nuts, fruits, and other foods you can offer birds to attract them. The most popular will depend on where you live and the types of birds visiting your feeders.

In addition to food, you can attract birds by providing water (sometimes running water, a mister or dripper, is necessary) and shelter.

Type of Bird	Food
Blue Jays and other Jays	Peanuts, sunflower seed, suet, cracked corn, bread products, peanut butter, lard & seed mixes
Cardinals and Grosbeaks	Sunflower seed, safflower, cracked corn, millet, apples and other fruit, peanuts
Cedar Waxwings	Berries, raisins, apple slices, currents, grapes
Goldfinches and other Finches	Sunflower seed, Nyjer (thistle), sunflower hearts, millet, fruit, suet, peanuts
Hummingbirds	Plant nectar from appropriate live plants, sugar solution
Indigo Buntings and other Buntings	Peanuts, millet, mixed seeds, sunflower hearts
Kinglets	Suet, suet mixes, baked products, mealworms
Mockingbirds, Thrashers, Catbirds	Halved apples, chopped fruits, mealworms, suet, nutmeats, millet (thrashers), soaked raisins, currents, sunflower hearts
Mourning Doves and other Doves	Millet, Nyjer (thistle), sunflower hearts, safflower, cracked corn

Type of Bird	Food
Nuthatches	Suet, suet mixes, sunflower seed, sunflower hearts, peanuts, peanut butter, mealworms
Orioles	Halved oranges, apples, berries, grape jelly, suet mixes, soaked raisins, mealworms, currents
Pine Siskins and other Siskins	Nuts, rolled oats, Nyjer (thistle), mixed seed, sunflower seed, sunflower hearts, millet, suet
Quail	Sunflower seed, seed mixes
Red-Winged Blackbirds	Cracked corn, mixed seed, sunflower seed, sunflower hearts, millet, suet, bread products
Robins, Bluebirds, and other Thrushes	Apples, sunflower seed, mealworms, berries, suet, chopped fruit, soaked raisins, currents, nutmeats, sunflower hearts
Tanagers	Suet, fruits, sugar solution, mealworms, baked products
Titmice and Chickadees	Peanuts, sunflower seed, suet, peanut butter, mealworms
Towhees and Juncos	Millet, sunflower seed, peanuts, cracked corn, suet, nutmeats, baked products
Warblers	Suet, suet mixes, fruit, baked products, sugar solution, chopped nutmeats
Woodpeckers	Suet, meat scraps, sunflower seed, sunflower hearts, cracked corn, peanuts, fruits, mealworms
Wrens and Creepers	Suet, suet mixes, peanut butter, peanuts, bread products, fruit, millet (wrens), mealworms

Bird Sighting Record

Date _____

Species/Description _____

_____

_____

Location _____

Notes _____

_____

_____

Date _____

Species/Description _____

_____

_____

Location _____

Notes _____

_____

_____

Date _____

Species/Description _____

_____

_____

Location _____

Notes _____

_____

_____

Date _____

Species/Description _____

_____

_____

Location _____

Notes _____

_____

_____

Date _____

Species/Description _____

_____

_____

Location _____

Notes _____

_____

_____

Date _____

Species/Description _____

_____

_____

Location _____

Notes _____

_____

_____

Date _____

Species/Description _____

_____

_____

Location _____

_____

Notes _____

_____

_____

Date _____

Species/Description _____

_____

_____

Location _____

_____

Notes _____

_____

_____

Date _____

Species/Description _____

_____

_____

Location _____

_____

Notes _____

_____

_____

Date _____

Species/Description _____

_____

_____

Location _____

_____

Notes _____

_____

_____

Date _____

Species/Description _____

_____

_____

Location _____

_____

Notes _____

_____

_____

Date _____

Species/Description _____

_____

_____

Location _____

_____

Notes _____

_____

_____

National Organizations for Bird Watchers

American Bird Conservatory
P. O. Box 249
4249 Loudoun Avenue
The Plains, VA 20198-2237
888-247-3624
www.abcbirds.org

American Birding Association
4945 N. 30th Street, Suite 200
Colorado Springs, CO 80919
800-850-2473
www.aba.org

Cornell Laboratory of Ornithology
159 Sapsucker Woods Road
Ithaca, NY 14850
800-843-2473
www.birds.cornell.edu

National Audubon Society
225 Varick Street
New York, NY 10014
212-979-3000
www.audubon.org

National Wildlife Federation
11100 Wildlife Center Drive
Reston, VA 20190-5362
800-822-9919
www.nwf.org

The Nature Conservancy
4245 North Fairfax Drive, Suite 100
Arlington, VA 22203-1606
800-628-6860
www.nature.org